Revised Edition

Ichiro Suzuki

By Jeff Savage

AMAZING ATHLETES

𝖑 **Lerner Publications Company • Minneapolis**

Lerner Publications Company
A division of Lerner Publishing Group
241 First Avenue North
Minneapolis, MN 55401 U.S.A.

Website address: www.lernerbooks.com

Library of Congress Cataloging-in-Publication Data

Savage, Jeff, 1961-
    Ichiro Suzuki / by Jeff Savage. — Rev. ed.
      p. cm. — (Amazing athletes)
    Includes bibliographical references and index.
    ISBN-13: 978-0-8225-7266-4 (lib. bdg. : alk. paper)
    ISBN-10: 0-8225-7266-4 (lib. bdg. : alk. paper)
    1. Suzuki, Ichiro, 1973- —Juvenile literature. 2. Baseball players—Japan—Biography—Juvenile literature. I. Title.
    GV865.S895.S38 2007
    796.357092—dc22
    [B]   2006022530

Manufactured in the United States of America
1 2 3 4 5 6 – DP – 12 11 10 09 08 07

TABLE OF CONTENTS

Before Ichiro goes to bat, he stretches his body.
He even exercises while he's in right field.

A FAST START

Ichiro Suzuki, a native of Japan, came to the
plate to bat for the Seattle Mariners at the
team's home field. Before stepping into the
batter's box, though, he did an exercise. He
slowly bent over at the waist. His face nearly

touched the ground. Ichiro does this motion to find balance.

The sellout crowd of 45,000 people watched Ichiro's ritual. In Japan, millions more watched on television. They had seen the motion before. He had just joined the Mariners at right field to become the first Japanese non-pitcher to enter Major League Baseball.

Japanese American fans show their support for Ichiro.

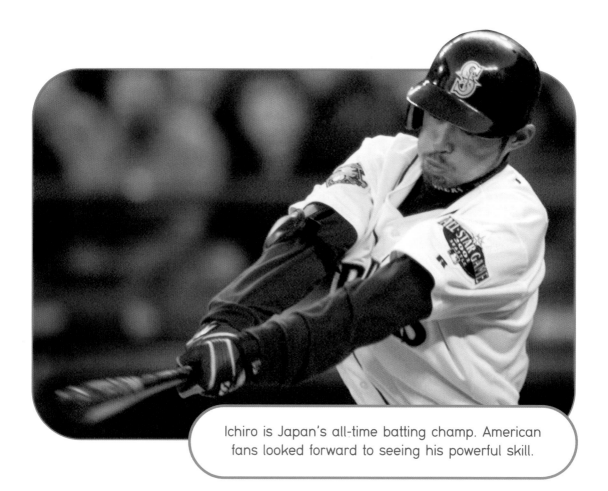

Ichiro is Japan's all-time batting champ. American fans looked forward to seeing his powerful skill.

Ichiro is quick! He can run from home plate to first base in 3.7 seconds.

More than 100 newspaper and TV reporters from Japan were in Seattle to see Ichiro's first game. They knew what Ichiro could do. Baseball fans in America were about to find out.

Ichiro made outs his first three times at bat. But in the seventh inning, Ichiro smashed a ball that whistled past the pitcher and into center field for a **single.** The Mariners were trailing the Oakland A's by one run, but not for long. On the next hit, Ichiro raced around the bases to score. The game was tied, 4–4.

After making a few outs, Ichiro got on base in the team's season opener against the Oakland A's.

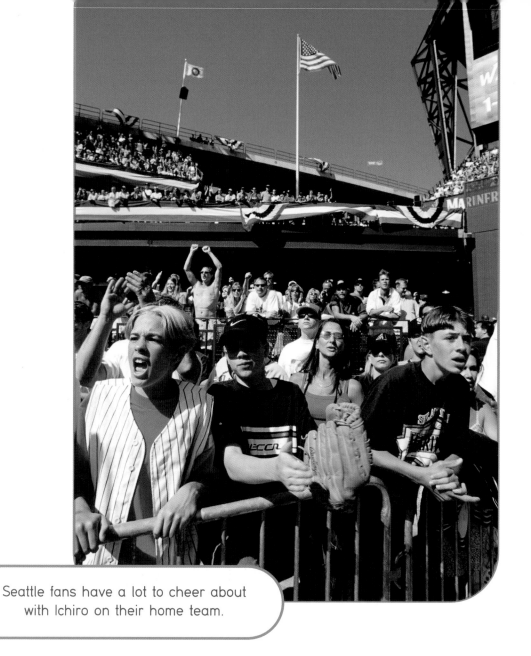

Seattle fans have a lot to cheer about
with Ichiro on their home team.

In the eighth inning, Carlos Guillen stood on
first base when Ichiro came to bat once more.
"EE-chee-ro! EE-chee-ro!" the fans chanted.

Ichiro responded by smartly **bunting** the ball down the **first-base line.** He blazed to first base so fast that the A's pitcher panicked and threw the ball away. Guillen eventually scored the winning run. The crowd cheered for Ichiro. He smiled and waved. Later, he told reporters, "The feelings I have tonight I will never forget."

Ichiro's bunt in the eighth inning helped the Mariners win their first game of the season.

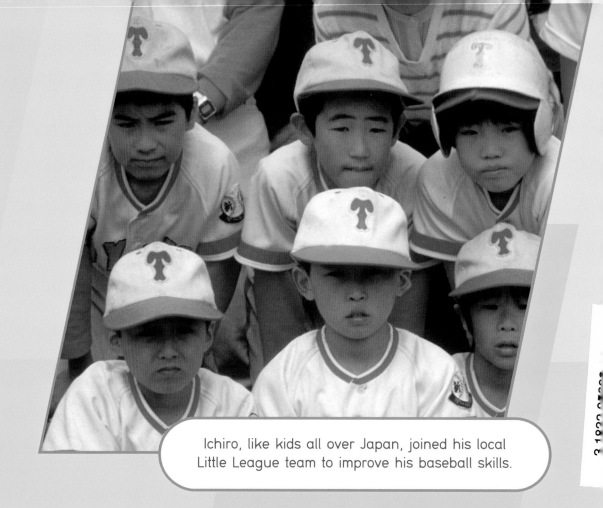

Ichiro, like kids all over Japan, joined his local Little League team to improve his baseball skills.

LEARNING THE GAME

Ichiro Suzuki was born October 22, 1973, in Kasugai, Japan. His first name is pronounced "ee-chee-ro." It means "first boy." Some say it also translates to "fast man."

Baseball is a popular sport in Japan, just as it is in America. Ichiro grew up in Nagoya and began playing with a baseball at age three. He rode his bicycle to elementary school and earned good grades. By second grade, he had completely fallen in love with baseball. He wanted to become a great player someday.

Japan, Ichiro's home country, is long and narrow. His hometown of Nagoya is a big port city in central Japan where cloth, bicycles, and other products are made.

Ichiro joined his hometown Little League team. His father, Nobuyuki, became coach of the team. The team played only on Sundays. Ichiro knew he would need to play more than once a week to become great. So he and his father practiced every day after school. Ichiro worked hard on fundamentals such as bunting, hitting, and baserunning.

An American schoolteacher introduced baseball to Japan in the 1870s. By the 1930s, the first professional Japanese leagues were in place. By the 1970s, when Ichiro started to become interested in baseball, the sport was well established.

Ichiro went to Aiko-Dai Meiden High School in Nagoya. He was a star on the school's baseball team. Twice he played in Koshien, the national high school baseball tournament in

Japan. He impressed Japanese professional **scouts.** Upon his graduation from high school, he was **drafted** by a team called the Orix Blue Wave as their right fielder.

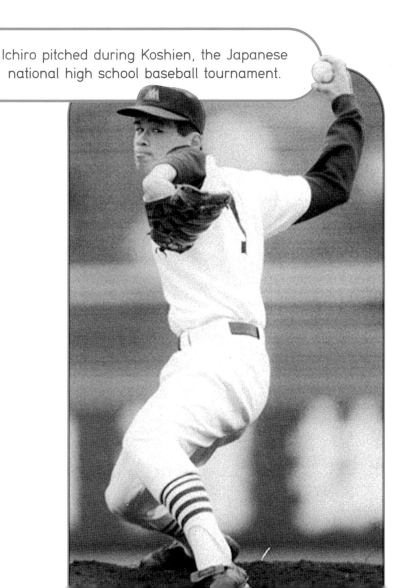

Ichiro pitched during Koshien, the Japanese national high school baseball tournament.

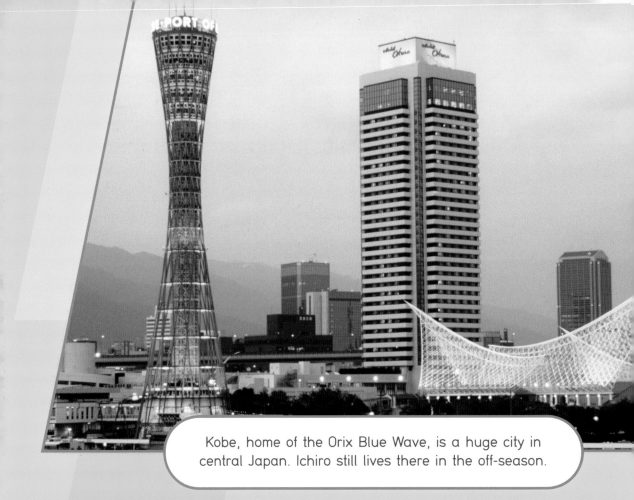

Kobe, home of the Orix Blue Wave, is a huge city in central Japan. Ichiro still lives there in the off-season.

TURNING PRO

Ichiro had achieved his dream. He had become a pro baseball player. The Blue Wave played their home games in Kobe, a port city of nearly two million people. But before Ichiro could join

the Blue Wave, he played in the **minor leagues.**
There he learned how to hit pro pitching and
perfected his sprint around the bases.

In 1993, Ichiro was called up to the Blue
Wave. He quickly became a
star in Japan. In Ichiro's
first full season, he set a
record with 210 hits. He
led the league in batting
average and was named
the 1994 Japanese Pacific
League's Most Valuable Player (MVP).

Ichiro improved
his blinding
speed around the
bases in the
minor leagues.

The next year, he led in batting average
again. He also ranked first in runs batted in
(RBI) and **stolen bases.** He was named league
MVP again. In 1996, he led the Blue Wave to
the Japan Series championship. He was an
easy choice as league MVP again.

With the Orix Blue Wave, Ichiro became an outstanding batter. He won the Japanese Pacific League's batting award seven times in a row.

Ichiro's style stood out in many ways. He threw from right field with his right hand, yet he batted left-handed.

In the batter's box, he aimed his bat toward the pitcher. He looked as if he was about to duel with a sword. He swung with quick wrists and a slashing swing.

Ichiro was equally skilled in the outfield of the Blue Wave team. Here, he slides to make a catch.

Ichiro followed up his hits with incredible running speed. He not only reached first base quickly but was often able to steal additional bases.

Upon making contact, Ichiro put on a burst of speed to reach first base. And in the outfield, Ichiro's ability to chase down balls was matched by his powerful throwing arm.

Ichiro had become the most popular baseball player in Japan. The team's souvenir shops sold Ichiro cups, key chains, baseballs, jerseys, T-shirts, posters, stickers, notebooks, pins, and flags. He was known throughout Japan simply as Ichiro. His coach even changed the name on the back of his uniform from Suzuki to Ichiro.

In a game against a team from Osaka, Japan, Ichiro made an incredible catch to save the game.

Ichiro thanked his many Japanese fans at his last game as a Blue Wave. He had decided to join the American major leagues.

AN INSTANT HIT

In 2000, Ichiro won the Japanese batting title for the seventh straight time. He had become so famous that a letter addressed simply to "Ichiro, Japan" would reach his mailbox. A poll named him the most recognizable person in Japan, just ahead of the emperor of Japan.

But Ichiro wanted to play baseball in North America, where baseball had begun. Many major league baseball teams wanted him. The Seattle Mariners offered the most money. They paid $13 million to the Blue Wave and $15 million to Ichiro. Ichiro was sad to leave Japan but excited to come to America. "I go, but another star soon will replace me," Ichiro said.

Ichiro was all smiles after signing his contract to play for the Seattle Mariners in December of 2000.

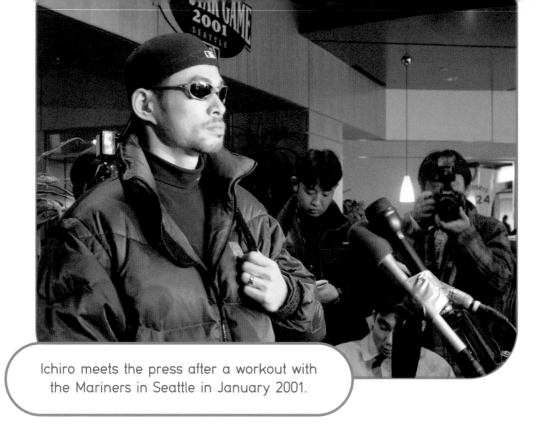

Ichiro meets the press after a workout with the Mariners in Seattle in January 2001.

When Ichiro joined the Mariners for the 2001 season, seven Japanese pitchers were on major league rosters. However, Ichiro became the first non-pitcher to join Major League Baseball. Some predicted that Ichiro would do well. Others thought he would be a bust. "Sometimes I am nervous, sometimes anxious," said Ichiro. "But I want to challenge a new world."

Ichiro was an instant hit. He had his first great game on Opening Day. A few days later, he hit a game-winning **home run** in extra innings. The next day, he made a laserlike throw from right field to nail a base runner at third base.

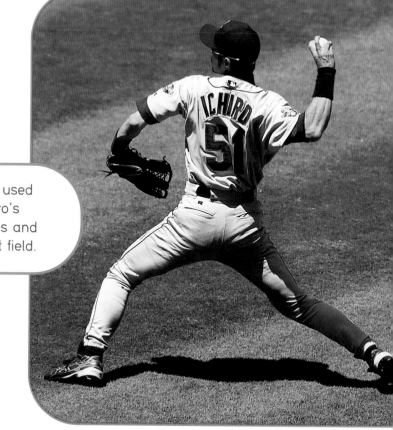

Seattle fans got used to seeing Ichiro's incredible catches and throws from right field.

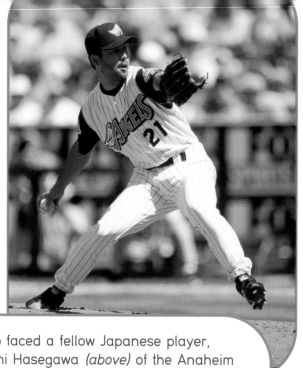

Ichiro faced a fellow Japanese player, Shigetoshi Hasegawa *(above)* of the Anaheim Angels, during his first season. Hasegawa later joined Ichiro on the Mariners team.

Two nights later, in a game against the Anaheim Angels, he singled off Shigetoshi Hasegawa. Hasegawa had been Ichiro's former teammate with the Orix Blue Wave. This was the first time an Asian batter faced an Asian pitcher in the major leagues. After Ichiro's single, the baseball was boxed up and sent to the National Baseball Hall of Fame.

The Mariners won 116 games to tie the major league record for most victories in one season. Ichiro hit .350 to win the league batting title. He also led the league in hits and stolen bases.

A player's batting average is arrived at by dividing the number of hits a player has by the number of times the player was at bat.

Stealing bases is another of Ichiro's strengths. He led the league in stolen bases in his rookie American year.

In the playoffs, he batted a record .600 to lead the Mariners past the Cleveland Indians in five games. Seattle was one step from reaching the World Series for the first time in its twenty-five-year history. But its magical season ended against the New York Yankees.

In 2001, Seattle reached the American League Championship. Here, Ichiro makes a sliding catch during a game against the New York Yankees. The Yankees eventually ended Seattle's 2001 season.

Ichiro receives a Gold Glove award for the 2005 season. He has won the award six times.

RECORD BREAKER

Ichiro continues to smash records. With his unshakeable play and sweet swing, he has proven himself to be one of the game's best players.

Ichiro has been named to the All Star Game in each of his Major League Baseball seasons.

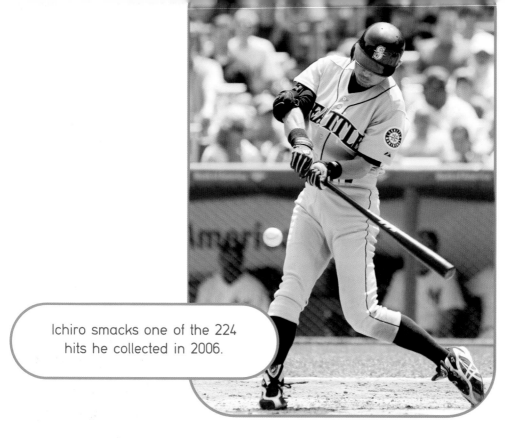

Ichiro smacks one of the 224 hits he collected in 2006.

He finished fourth in the league in batting in 2002 with a .321 average. In 2003 he became only the third major league player to record more than 200 hits in each of his first three seasons.

The 2004 season proved to be Ichiro's best yet. He set the all-time record for most hits in a year with 262. The previous record had stood since 1920! Ichiro didn't slow down in 2005. He again collected more than 200 hits and won another Gold Glove award for his fielding. In 2006, Ichiro again smacked over 200 hits and continued his sparkling outfield play.

The Mariners' star right fielder has continued to shine. The team has not made the playoffs since 2001, but there will be more chances for the Mariners with Ichiro leading the way. He has become a national hero in *two* countries.

Ichiro likes to play golf. He is able to play often in the United States. That isn't the case when he's in Japan. "I can't play in Japan because every golf course has caddies," Ichiro explained. "The caddies all want autographs and don't want to let me play golf."

Selected Career Highlights

2006   collected 200 or more hits for seventh straight season
led Majors in hits
won his sixth Gold Glove award

2005   won his fifth Gold Glove award

2004   led Majors in hits
set all-time record (262) for hits in a season

2003   finished second in hits in American League

2002   won his second Gold Glove award
led Majors in All-Star ballotting for second year

2001   won American League batting title
won his first Gold Glove award
led the American League in stolen bases
named American League's Most Valuable Player
named American League's Rookie of the Year

2000   won seventh straight Japanese Pacific League batting title

1999   won sixth straight Japanese Pacific League batting title

1998   won fifth straight Japanese Pacific League batting title

1997   won fourth straight Japanese Pacific League batting title

1996   named Japanese Pacific League's Most Valuable Player
won third straight Japanese Pacific League batting title

1995   named Japanese Pacific League's Most Valuable Player
won second straight Japanese Pacific League batting title

1994   named Japanese Pacific League's Most Valuable Player
won Japanese Pacific League batting title

Glossary

batter's box: the rectangular area next to home plate in which the batter stands

bunt: a short hit that doesn't involve swinging the bat. Bunting surprises the opposing players and advances a teammate already on base.

draft: a yearly event in which all professional teams in a major league sport are given the chance to pick new players from a selected group. Most of the players in the group have played their sport in college.

first-base line: the white chalk line that extends from home plate to first base. Inside the line, a batted ball is fair or in play. Outside the line, a batted ball is foul and not in play.

home run: a play in which the batter hits the ball and circles the bases safely to cross home plate

minor leagues: the lower leagues where young players improve their playing skills. It is one step below the major leagues.

scout: a person who reviews the playing skills of young players

single: a play in which the batter hits the ball and safely reaches first base

stolen base: an act in which a runner on base advances to the next base without aid

Further Reading & Websites

Leigh, David S. *Ichiro Suzuki*. Minneapolis: Twenty-First Century Books, 2004.

Rappoport, Ken. *Super Sports Star Ichiro Suzuki*. Berkeley Heights, NJ: Enslow Publishers, Inc., 2004.

Stewart, Mark. *Ichiro Suzuki: Best in the West*. Minneapolis: Lerner Publications Company, 2002.

Collectibles Website
http://www.ichirocollectables.com
A fan website that has Ichiro memorabilia such as posters, pennants, and autographed baseballs.

Ichiro Trading Cards
http://www.ichirorookies.com
A website that tells all about Ichiro's trading cards.

Official MLB Site
http://www.mlb.com
The official Major League Baseball website that provides fans with game action, biographies of players, and information about baseball.

Sports Illustrated for Kids
http://www.sikids.com
The *Sports Illustrated for Kids* website that covers all sports, including baseball.

Index

Photo Acknowledgments

Photographs are used with the permission of: © Michael
Zito/SportsChrome, pp. 4, 23; © Reuters NewMedia, Inc./CORBIS, pp. 5, 6, 30;
© AFP/Getty Images, pp. 7, 22; © Natalie Fobes/CORBIS, p. 8; © Otto Greule
Jr./Getty Images, pp. 9, 26, 27; © Robert Holmes/CORBIS, p. 10; © Steve
Kaufman/CORBIS, p. 11; © Kyodo News Agency, pp. 13, 16, 17, 18, 19, 20, 21;
© Michael S. Yamashita/CORBIS, p. 14; © Jeff Gross/Getty Images, p. 24; ©
Rob Tringali/SportsChrome, p. 25; © Jim McIsaac/Getty Images, p. 28.

Cover: © Otto Greule Jr./Getty Images.